FLORIDA
GATORS

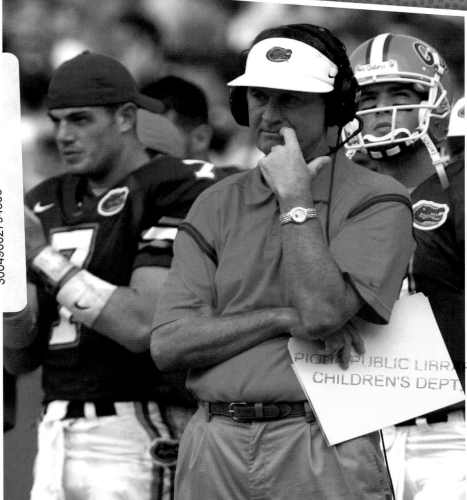

BY MARTY GITLIN

Published by ABDO Publishing Company, PO Box 398166, Minneapolis, MN 55439. Copyright © 2013 by Abdo Consulting Group, Inc. International copyrights reserved in all countries. No part of this book may be reproduced in any form without written permission from the publisher. SportsZone™ is a trademark and logo of ABDO Publishing Company.

Printed in the United States of America,
North Mankato, Minnesota
052012
092012

 THIS BOOK CONTAINS AT LEAST 10% RECYCLED MATERIALS.

Editor: Chrös McDougall
Series Designer: Craig Hinton

Photo Credits: Scott A. Miller/AP Images, cover; Peter Cosgrove/AP Images, 1; Paul Spinelli/AP Images, 4; Charles Krupa/AP Images, 7; John Amis/AP Images, 9; Mark J. Terrill/AP Images, 10, 43 (bottom); State Archives of Florida, 12, 42 (top); John Lindsay/AP Images, 17, 43 (top left); AP Images, 18, 29; Bettmann/Corbis/AP Images, 21, 43 (top right); Florida/Collegiate Images/Getty Images, 23, 26, 42 (bottom left); Sporting News/Getty Images, 24; Scott Halleran/Allsport/Getty Images, 31; John Bazmore/AP Images, 32, 37, 42 (bottom right); Chris O'Meara/AP Images, 34; John Raoux/AP Images, 39; Phelan M. Ebenhack/AP Images, 40, 44

Library of Congress Cataloging-in-Publication Data
Gitlin, Marty.
  Florida Gators / by Marty Gitlin.
      p. cm. -- (Inside college football)
  Includes index.
  ISBN 978-1-61783-496-7
  1. University of Florida--Football--History--Juvenile literature. 2. Florida Gators (Football team)--History--Juvenile literature. I. Title.
  GV958.U523G58 2013
  796.332'630975979--dc23
                              2012001849

TABLE OF CONTENTS

DEC 2012

Coach Urban Meyer led Florida to the 2006 national championship in just his second year as the Gators' coach.

RUNNING AWAY WITH A CROWN

THE UNIVERSITY OF FLORIDA GATORS FOOTBALL TEAM WAS PREPARING TO FACE THE OHIO STATE BUCKEYES IN THE 2006 BOWL CHAMPIONSHIP SERIES (BCS) NATIONAL CHAMPIONSHIP GAME. THE SHOWDOWN WAS SET FOR JANUARY 8, 2007.

Gators coach Urban Meyer had an idea for motivating his players. He placed a huge bulletin board in the locker room during the week before the game. On it, he posted articles written about the team. Some articles predicted Ohio State would easily win. Others featured so-called experts claiming the Gators could not match up to the talented Buckeyes.

Meyer later referred to the board as "10 feet of nonsense." That is because some items he placed on it were pure fiction. They were created simply to make his players angry. Meyer's plan worked. The players grew angrier as the showdown approached. Meyer worked to make the Gators believe they were better than Ohio State.

GATORS

OHIO'S OWN

Urban Meyer led Florida to the 2006 national title over the team he rooted for growing up. Meyer was born and raised in Ohio. In fact, when he was younger, he hoped to someday play for the Buckeyes. Meyer even began his coaching career at Ohio State. And in 2011, he was finally named the Buckeyes' coach.

Meyer grew up in the town of Ashtabula, Ohio. He starred in baseball growing up. Boyhood buddy Dean Hood told one story that showed Meyer's competitive nature. Hood recalled watching Meyer play one brilliant game as both a hitter and a fielder. But Meyer made an out in the last inning. He was so upset that he refused a ride home from Hood. Hood was stunned. After all, Meyer lived 5 miles (8 km) away.

Meyer attempted to play professional baseball. However, he soon turned to coaching football. He guided Utah to back-to-back bowl game wins before taking the job at Florida in 2005.

Gators junior defensive end Jarvis Moss required no convincing. "We were such a tight team and had our own identity," he said. "We knew who we were and what Ohio State was. Our coaches didn't have to convince us we could beat Ohio State. I think everybody on our team knew we were better than Ohio State and faster than them before we even played the game."

Ohio State did boast one lightning-fast player in wide receiver Ted Ginn Jr. He showed off that speed on the opening kickoff. Ginn returned it 93 yards for a touchdown.

Meyer believed his team needed to answer with a touchdown on the next drive. And that is what the Gators did. Senior quarterback Chris Leak threw a touchdown pass to senior wide receiver Dallas Baker to tie the game. After that, the Gators never looked back.

Standout freshman wide receiver Percy Harvin scored a touchdown on a short run just minutes later in the

Florida freshman quarterback Tim Tebow prepares to throw in the first half of the 2007 national championship game.

first quarter. And senior running back DeShawn Wynn added another touchdown on the first play of the second quarter. That stretched the Gators' lead to 21–7.

But the Buckeyes were not ready to give up. They came back four plays later with a touchdown. Then Florida responded with two field goals. And Moss took matters into his own hands. He sacked Ohio State quarterback Troy Smith, who fumbled the ball. The Gators recovered on Ohio State's 5-yard line.

Meyer sent Florida's dual-threat freshman quarterback Tim Tebow onto the field. Tebow would eventually become an all-time great for the Gators. As a freshman, he was mainly used in spot situations to try to confuse defenses. In this situation, Meyer called for a passing play. And Tebow completed a pass to junior wide receiver Andre Caldwell for the touchdown. That put Florida up 34–14 at halftime. The play capped a stunning first half against what had been a powerful defense in Ohio State.

Florida added one more touchdown in the second half. It was enough to secure a dominating 41–14 victory. After the game, Meyer held the crystal trophy above his head. Then he passed it to Leak. The senior planted a big kiss on the trophy. He had finished his college career as a champion. Florida was the number one team in the nation.

The college football world was stunned. Many were surprised that Florida won. That the Gators won by 27 points was even more amazing. But Baker was among the many Florida players who expected a victory.

"I'm not surprised at all," he said while his teammates celebrated. "We had something to prove. Some people were predicting Ohio State to win 41–14. Well, it was 41–14 for the University of Florida. Nobody gave us a chance. Now, we can finally throw up a number one. We had a lot of doubters out there, the media, the Ohio State fans. No one can doubt us now. We're national champs."

Florida quarterback Chris Leak pitches the ball to wide receiver Percy Harvin during the 2006 SEC title game.

Florida proved it was worthy of that ranking throughout the year. The Gators play in the Southeastern Conference (SEC). Many considered it to be the toughest football conference in 2006. Including Florida, six SEC teams were ranked among the nation's top 25 that year. The Gators beat four of them. Florida's only loss came against the Auburn Tigers. Auburn finished the season ranked ninth.

The SEC championship came down to a showdown that matched Florida against eighth-ranked Arkansas. The game could have been called "The Percy Harvin Show." The freshman wide receiver caught six passes for 105 yards and a touchdown. He also took a handoff and ran 67 yards

Florida quarterback Chris Leak holds the trophy after leading the Gators to the 2007 BCS National Championship Game title.

for a touchdown early in the fourth quarter. That gave the fourth-ranked Gators a 31–21 lead.

The Razorbacks answered quickly with a touchdown. But Florida used more trickery to again break away. Caldwell was not a quarterback. However, he tossed a touchdown strike to junior tight end Tate Casey.

That put the Gators 10 points ahead. Arkansas never recovered.

Still, Florida was not guaranteed a spot in the national title game. The Gators learned during halftime that the second-ranked University of Southern California (USC) Trojans had lost. Top-ranked Ohio State was certain to be in the title game. But the BCS committee had to decide who would face the Buckeyes. Michigan had been ranked higher than Florida. But the Wolverines had already lost to Ohio State that year.

"We're going to tell a group of young men who just went 12–1 with the most difficult schedule against six ranked opponents that they don't have a chance to play for a national championship?" Meyer asked in wonderment.

But nobody had to tell that to the Gators. They jumped ahead of Michigan in the rankings and earned a berth in the national title game. And the Gators knew they would beat Ohio State—even if nobody else did.

GATORS GLORY

Florida beat Ohio State to become the national champions in football in January 2007. Nine months earlier, the Gators also won the men's basketball championship. The school became the first to capture the title in both sports in the same year. Three months after Florida and Ohio State faced off for the football title, the two schools faced off in the basketball championship game. Florida won this one as well, claiming back-to-back titles.

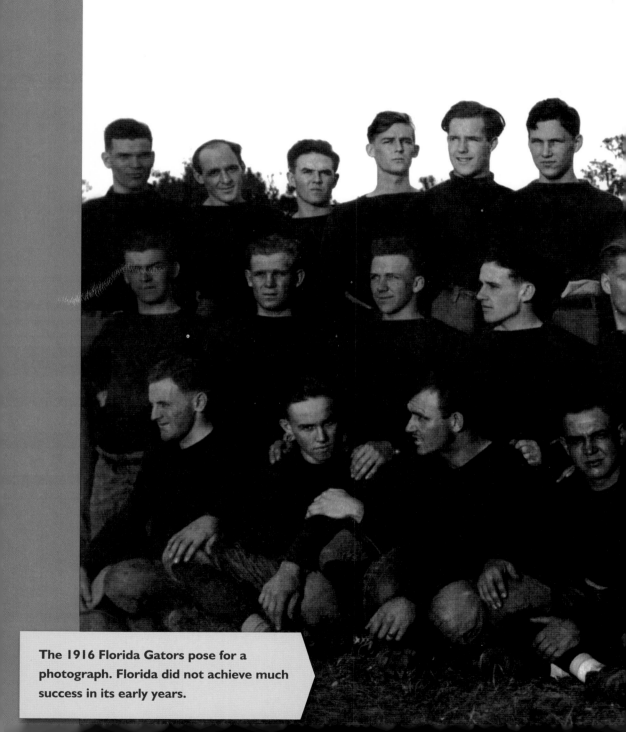

The 1916 Florida Gators pose for a photograph. Florida did not achieve much success in its early years.

THE GROWING GATORS

IT WAS NOVEMBER 22, 1901. PEOPLE THROUGHOUT THE UNITED STATES WERE PREPARING FOR THANKSGIVING. AND THE FLORIDA AGRICULTURAL COLLEGE FOOTBALL TEAM WAS PLAYING ITS FIRST GAME.

The showdown was against nearby Stetson College. The *Florida Times-Union* newspaper wrote highly of the game. It referred to football as a "royal game" that tests "the best resources, the pluck, the endurance, and speed of lusty young manhood."

The game, however, was no thing of beauty. The team described during its earliest days as "the Blue and White" lost 6–0 to Stetson. The outcome might have been different had one sure touchdown pass not hit a tree stump on the field.

The school was renamed the University of Florida in 1903. It adopted the Gators nickname five years later. But those changes did not bring more victories. One early

HITCHHIKING TO GLORY

Charlie LaPradd yearned to play for Florida. He still had that dream after surviving dangerous missions as a paratrooper in World War II. So he hitchhiked to Florida in 1949 and asked for a chance to play.

Coach Bob Woodruff provided him with an opportunity. And LaPradd blossomed into an All-American. He starred as both an offensive and defensive lineman. LaPradd is still considered one of the finest players in the history of the program.

"[He] was extremely tough," said teammate Joe D'Agostino. "It took two or three men to get him out of the way. They couldn't move him. He was our team captain, and he kept up the spirit on the line. He'd come up and down the line, hitting us on the butt and telling us to get with it and play hard, and we all loved him."

LaPradd later coached the Florida State freshman team to two undefeated seasons.

Florida team lost to Alabama, Auburn, Georgia, and Georgia Tech by a combined score of 201–0.

Florida joined the Southern Intercollegiate Athletic Association in 1912. The Gators had seven winning records in the next 10 years. But they finished just 0–5 in 1916, scoring only three points all season. The yearbook staff took a more positive spin on the season. It wrote: "They have the admiration and satisfaction of a loyal student body that supported them through all the trials and troubles of defeat."

A new era started in 1922 when Florida joined the Southern Conference. The Gators had eight winning seasons out of 11. They peaked in 1928, going 8–1 under coach Charlie Bachman. That year, they led the nation in scoring. Junior end Dale Van Sickel also became Florida's first All-American player.

The defense shined that season. Florida gave up seven points or less in each of its first eight games. Then it lost 13–12 against Tennessee. That loss prevented the Gators from finishing undefeated. It also prevented them from landing a berth in the Rose Bowl. The Rose Bowl is the oldest and some say most prestigious bowl game.

Florida followed that season by going 8–2 in 1929. But as the United States fell into the Great Depression, so did the Gators. They joined the SEC in 1933. And they had just one winning season from 1935 to 1951. Even then, they only finished 4–3 that year, in 1944.

The school did not make football a priority during those times. Money was tight during the Great Depression. Then the United States entered World War II in 1941. So many young men were fighting in Europe and Asia that Florida did not field a team in 1943.

"The University of Florida did not emphasize the team during [the 1930s and early 1940s], like Alabama and some of the others," said Bill Mills Sr., who was friends with some Florida players.

NEW PLACE TO PLAY

The Gators did not have a steady home during their early years. They played many home games at Fleming Field on their campus in Gainesville. But they also hosted opponents in Jacksonville, St. Petersburg, Tampa, and even Miami. That finally changed in 1930. A group led by University President John J. Tigert funded the construction of Florida Field. The facility opened on November 8. However, during its inaugural game, the Gators lost 20–0 to Alabama before 21,000 fans. Florida Field at Ben Hill Griffin Stadium remains the team's home stadium.

The Gators simply could not compete during that period in the tough SEC. They had an 18–60–5 record against league opponents from 1935 to 1951. And they won no more than one SEC game in every year from 1941 to 1947. Fuller Warren was running for governor of the state in 1948. He mentioned the Gators' woes during a speech.

"Next to my pledge to try to get the cows outlawed from public highways," he said, "my pledge to try and get that winning football team at Florida seemed to get the most applause."

The state passed a bill that sent money earned through gambling to the Florida football program. The next step was hiring 34-year-old coach Bob Woodruff away from Baylor in 1950. Woodruff demanded what was then a huge salary of $17,000 per year.

Florida did improve under Woodruff. But the team still did not win any conference or national titles. The Gators got a boost in 1950, when talented quarterback Haywood Sullivan chose to attend Florida. He threw for more than 2,000 yards in two seasons. But the Gators went just 5–5 in each of those years. Then Sullivan left the school to pursue a career in Major League Baseball.

The Gators actually enjoyed better results in 1952. They won eight games. Florida capped its season with a 14–13 win over Tulsa in the Gator Bowl. That was Florida's first appearance in a bowl game. But that 1952 season would be the only standout year under Woodruff. He coached Florida for 10 seasons. Yet only the 1952 squad won more than six games. Woodruff was fired after the 1959 season.

"[Woodruff] told me that for him to stay he had to [get] rid of some assistant coaches, but he wouldn't do it," Florida star quarterback Jimmy Dunn said. "He wouldn't fire them. . . . Those guys had been loyal to him, and he was extremely loyal to them. He wouldn't have any part in firing them, so they decided to [fire Woodruff]."

The bottom line was that Woodruff did not win enough games to save himself or his assistants. But that would not be a problem for Ray Graves. He replaced Woodruff as coach in 1960. And Graves was about to raise the Gators to new heights.

Florida coach Ray Graves speaks with his players in 1965. Graves installed an exciting offense upon arriving in 1960.

PUTTING FLORIDA FOOTBALL ON THE MAP

RAY GRAVES TOOK OVER AS FLORIDA'S HEAD FOOTBALL COACH IN 1960. HE KNEW WHAT HE NEEDED TO WIN: BETTER PLAYERS. RECRUITING THOSE PLAYERS WAS EASIER SAID THAN DONE, HOWEVER.

The Gators had been winners at times. But they had never contended for a national title. They had rarely even been a threat to win the SEC title. Graves was known as a great defensive coach from his time as an assistant with Georgia Tech. He also dumped the boring offense used by previous coach Bob Woodruff. Graves created an option attack. It gave the quarterback the choice between running and passing the ball. The offense also featured players in motion in hopes of confusing defenses.

Graves also wasted no time improving the Gators' defense. Florida ranked eleventh in the country in 1960 by allowing just 7.8 points per game. The team went 9–2 that

GATORS

GATORADE

The popular drink Gatorade was created at the University of Florida and named after its sports teams. The football team asked a group of university doctors in 1965 why the heat was taking such a physical toll on the players. Later studies revealed that the players were losing fluids that were not being replaced. So the doctors created a new drink that would replenish what was lost during intense exercise. They named it "Gatorade."

The new drink was credited for keeping the players fresher than their opponents in 1965 and 1966. The result was nine victories and a spot in the Orange Bowl. Word of the new drink eventually spread to college football programs across the country. Gatorade was even said to have played a role in the success of the 1969 Kansas City Chiefs. The Chiefs upset the heavily favored Minnesota Vikings in the Super Bowl that season.

season. It was the first time Florida had won nine games in a season. The Gators won their last four games, beating rival Georgia along the way. And Florida capped off the season with a 13–12 victory over Baylor in the Gator Bowl.

The coach had brought a sense of fun and achievement to his players. Quarterback Larry Libertore recalled how the new offense thrilled his teammates.

"I can remember in 1960 the look on the face of the players in the huddle of the excitement and the enthusiasm when I would call the play," Libertore said.

Florida fell to 4–5–1 the next year. But the squad continued improving after that. Star high school quarterback Steve Spurrier joined Florida in 1964. The team finally had a top quarterback. Spurrier passed for 3,905 yards and 30 touchdowns combined in 1965 and 1966. The Gators went 7–4 and then 9–2 in those years.

Florida was ranked among the top 10 teams in the country through most of those seasons. Spurrier was at his best as a senior in 1966. He became the first Florida player to win the Heisman Trophy that year. It is given annually to the best player in college football.

Spurrier led the Gators to their first Orange Bowl that season. The Orange Bowl is one of the most important bowl games each year. Florida faced off against Georgia Tech on January 2, 1967. A sore arm slowed down Spurrier. But sophomore halfback Larry Smith picked up the offense. He rushed for 187 yards. That included a 94-yard run.

Meanwhile, the defense held the Georgia Tech quarterbacks to just eight completions in 22 attempts. Florida won the game 27–12.

After the game, Graves spoke about a new era of success for Gators football. "A lot of people wondered if Florida was a big enough team for this kind of a bowl game, and I think we showed we are," he said.

Spurrier was not able to bring Florida its first national title during his time there as a player. But the team was on the rise when he left. And the winning seasons continued in Gainesville.

A trio of sophomores starred on the 1969 squad. They were quarterback John Reaves, wide receiver Carlos Alvarez, and future National Football League (NFL) superstar defensive end Jack Youngblood. Together they stunned seventh-ranked Houston in the season opener. They then won their first six games.

Florida soared to the seventh spot in the national rankings. But a midseason loss to Auburn and a tie against Georgia ended the Gators' national championship dreams. Reaves believed his Gators should have finished the year unbeaten.

GREATEST GATOR DEFENDER?

Some consider defensive end Jack Youngblood to be the best defensive player in Florida history. He led the 1969 team with 66 tackles and earned All-American honors the following year. But Youngblood performed even better in the NFL. He played 14 seasons for the Los Angeles Rams. Youngblood earned a spot in the Pro Bowl every season from 1973 to 1979. He was inducted into the Pro Football Hall of Fame in 2001.

Reaves was not the only one who considered the 1969 season a disappointment. As such, Graves was fired. Former Gators quarterback Doug Dickey replaced him. Dickey had just guided Tennessee to an SEC title. He could not do the same at Florida, though. He stayed at Florida for nine seasons. Yet only his 1975 squad finished better than tied for third in the SEC.

Wide receiver Wes Chandler helped Florida to a strong three-year run surrounding that 1975 season. In 1974, the Gators sprinted to a 7–1 start and rose to number six in the national rankings. But they ended up finishing just 8–4 and losing to Nebraska in the Sugar Bowl. The 1975 squad went 9–3 but was shut out by Maryland in the Gator Bowl.

PUTTING FLORIDA FOOTBALL ON THE MAP

Florida wide receiver Cris Collinsworth caught 120 passes for 1,937 yards and 14 touchdowns from 1978 to 1980.

Florida then went 8–4 in Chandler's junior season of 1976. However, at the Sun Bowl, Texas A&M handed Florida its third consecutive loss in a bowl game.

Florida slipped to 6–4–1 in 1977 and 4–7 in 1978. Former Clemson coach Charley Pell replaced Dickey after that. But the coaching change did little to help the results on the field. Three early injuries destroyed Florida's 1979 season. All-American senior linebacker Scot Brantley and his brother, quarterback John Brantley, were injured in the second game. Talented sophomore defensive lineman David Galloway was lost in the first game. The Gators never recovered. They finished 0–10–1. It was the first time the program failed to win a game since 1946. Through 2011, Florida only has four winless seasons.

"We never seemed to get a break," said junior quarterback Larry Oschab. "The ball always seemed to bounce against us."

Thanks to Pell, the ball would soon start bouncing their way. He worked to raise money and rebuild the entire football program. He improved the weight-training program. And he hired an assistant coach named Mike Shanahan. He would turn the Gators into an offensive power.

The Gators were about to go from one of the worst teams in college football to one of the best.

COLLINSWORTH: WORTH PLENTY

Cris Collinsworth was recruited as a quarterback at Florida but was quickly moved to wide receiver. It turned out to be a good move. Collinsworth caught 120 passes for 1,937 yards and 14 touchdowns from 1978 to 1980. And he just kept catching passes in the NFL. He had more than 1,000 receiving yards as a rookie with the Cincinnati Bengals. He matched the feat three more times in his career. Collinsworth also earned three trips to the Pro Bowl. Today he is a popular NFL broadcaster for NBC.

PUTTING FLORIDA FOOTBALL ON THE MAP

All-American linebacker Wilber Marshall led Florida's defense from 1980 to 1983.

4

GRIDIRON GREATS IN GAINESVILLE

NO COLLEGE FOOTBALL TEAM HAD EVER SPORTED A WINLESS RECORD ONE SEASON AND QUALIFIED FOR A BOWL GAME AFTER THE NEXT SEASON. THAT IS, IT NEVER HAPPENED UNTIL THE FLORIDA GATORS DID IT IN 1980.

Florida won six of its first seven games that season. That earned the Gators a spot in the top 20. The team eventually finished 8–4 after beating Maryland in the Tangerine Bowl. Behind a strong defense, Florida continued to improve in the years that followed. All-American linebacker Wilber Marshall led the way.

There was a problem, though. Florida was winning more games. But the Gators struggled to win big games. Florida started the 1983 season 6–0–1 and reached the number-five ranking. Then the Gators lost two in a row against the higher ranked teams of Auburn and Georgia. Coach Charley Pell's days appeared numbered after that.

"PIT BULL" MARSHALL

Florida star linebacker Wilber Marshall earned the nickname "Pit Bull" when he was playing in the NFL. He had 100 or more tackles six times and earned Pro Bowl honors three times in his 12-year career. But the violence of the sport took a brutal toll on his body. "I've got to have my knees replaced and both shoulders," he said in 2007. "I can't raise my arms over my shoulders. . . . I've had four knee surgeries. . . . I fractured both ankles. I've got nerve impairments in my wrists and hands. My spine is compressed and I've got bulging discs."

Pell's fate was sealed early in 1984. The National Collegiate Athletic Association (NCAA) charged the program with 107 violations. The charges ranged from illegal recruiting practices to payment of athletes. The NCAA even charged Pell with spying on his SEC rivals. The Gators got off to a 1–1–1 start under Pell that season. But he was fired after that and replaced by offensive coordinator Galen Hall.

Most people expected Florida to struggle in the wake of the violations. Instead, the 1984 squad became arguably the best Florida team to date. The Gators rolled over their next seven opponents. That included wins over eleventh-ranked Auburn, eighth-ranked Georgia, and twelfth-ranked Florida State.

With a 9–1–1 record, the Gators won their first SEC title. They climbed all the way up to number three in the nation. However, Florida was not allowed to play in a bowl game that year as a consequence from the NCAA. Then that spring, the SEC voted to void Florida's conference

Florida running back Emmitt Smith runs through defenders during a 1987 game against UCLA.

title due to the violations. The conference also decided Florida would not be eligible to win the SEC title in 1985 or 1986.

Still, Florida became known as a winning team. As such, many great players decided to play there in the years that followed. Among them was running back Emmitt Smith. As a freshman in 1987, Smith ran for 1,341 yards and 13 touchdowns. He averaged nearly six yards per carry. Smith peaked during his junior season with 1,599 yards rushing and 14 touchdowns. He was named SEC Player of the Year.

"I've been around a lot of great players, but [Smith] made unbelievable plays, and he made them look ordinary," Gators senior quarterback

TWO BACKS, ONE ROUND

Florida running backs John L. Williams and Neal Anderson were both taken in the first round of the 1986 NFL Draft. It marked the first time since 1971 that two running backs from the same school were selected in the opening round. Anderson performed particularly well during his professional career. He recorded three 1,000-plus-yard seasons with the Chicago Bears.

Kerwin Bell said in 1987. "Because Emmitt wasn't flashy at all. He had a great ability to make people miss him and also break tackles."

Smith was known as one of the best running backs in college football. But he could not turn the Gators into national championship contenders. They continued to have winning seasons. However, they never won quite enough to play in big-time bowl games.

The 1989 season was particularly rocky. The Gators started 4–1 under Hall. But the NCAA was preparing to again punish Florida for illegal activities. So Hall resigned, and the Gators finished 7–5.

The school hired former Florida All-American quarterback Steve Spurrier to take over as coach in 1990. But the new coach would have to work without Smith. The star running back decided to leave school early to enter the NFL Draft.

Even without Smith, the Gators improved in 1990. Spurrier developed a strong passing attack led by quarterback Shane Matthews. The sophomore threw for 2,952 yards and 23 touchdowns. The Gators

Florida quarterback Shane Matthews throws a pass during a 1992 game against Kentucky.

scored at least 27 points in 9 of 11 games. Florida's 6–1 conference record would have won the SEC title. But the Gators were not eligible due to the NCAA violations.

Florida fans did not have to wait long to get that first official league title, though. The 1991 squad was the first in school history to win 10

games. And that year, Matthews won his second straight SEC Player of the Year Award.

The highlight of the year was a showdown against the rival Florida State Seminoles in the final regular-season game. One of Florida's touchdowns came on a 72-yard pass from Matthews to sophomore wide receiver Harrison Houston. Meanwhile, Florida's defense stopped Florida State twice on the goal line. That helped the fifth-ranked Gators defeat the third-ranked Seminoles 14–9.

The low score seemed a bit unusual. After all, Matthews had already thrown for more than 3,000 yards that season. And the Gators had scored at least 31 points in five straight games. But Spurrier was not complaining.

"I told some coaches . . . that never in my life did I think I'd win a 14–9 game," he said. "But we won, and it's just as good as 44–9."

Florida moved up to number three in the country. However, the season ended on a sour note. Eighteenth-ranked Notre Dame upset Florida 39–28 in the Sugar Bowl. But it was hard for Florida fans to complain too much. Spurrier had turned the Gators into a national power. He had also helped clean up the program off the field.

The golden era of Gator football was just beginning. And the team's first national championship was right around the corner.

GREAT GATOR, GREATER COWBOY

Emmitt Smith blossomed into one of the top college football players at Florida. Few were surprised when he quickly became a star in the NFL. But nobody could have predicted that he would retire as arguably the best running back of all time. After all, Smith was not particularly fast or strong. But he powered through holes and worked for every yard.

Sixteen picks were made in the 1989 NFL Draft before the Dallas Cowboys finally took him at number 17. They never regretted it. Smith was no doubt talented. But he also became known for his reliability and toughness. He set an NFL record by rushing for more than 1,000 yards for 11 straight years.

Smith led the league in rushing four times and in rushing touchdowns three times. He finished his career with a league-record 18,355 rushing yards. Smith was enshrined into the Pro Football Hall of Fame in 2010.

Florida quarterback Danny Wuerffel hurls a touchdown pass during a 1995 game against rival Florida State.

5

THE CHAMPIONSHIP ERA

COACH STEVE SPURRIER HAD QUICKLY TURNED FLORIDA INTO ONE OF THE COUNTRY'S TOP PROGRAMS. BUT UNTIMELY LOSSES SEEMED TO DOOM THE TEAM EACH SEASON.

Several of those losses came against rival Florida State. Florida was 9–1 going into the 1993 showdown with Florida State. But the top-ranked Seminoles beat the seventh-ranked Gators 33–21. The two rivals played twice in 1994. Florida was again 9–1 when they met first. But this time the fourth-ranked Gators and the seventh-ranked Seminoles tied 31–31.

After Florida beat Alabama in the SEC Championship Game, the Gators and the Seminoles again met in the Sugar Bowl. Florida State came out on top this time, winning 23–17.

Florida finally got past Florida State in 1995. In fact, the Gators got past everybody during that regular season. Only one team was ranked higher than the undefeated Gators going into the bowl games. And that Nebraska Cornhuskers

THE SPURRIER STORY

Steve Spurrier was known for his enthusiasm. Some believed he was immature and went overboard by yelling at referees. But there was no doubt that he had turned the Gators into a national power. However, he came to regret his decision to leave Florida. Spurrier's Washington Redskins went just 12–20 in two seasons. There were rumors that he might come back to Florida after that. Instead, he took the same position at South Carolina in 2005. He coached the Gamecocks to a 55–35 record in his first seven seasons there.

team beat Florida 62–24 in the Fiesta Bowl.

The 1995 season marked the closest Florida had been to winning a national title. The Gators then started the 1996 season 10–0. But a loss to Florida State in the regular-season finale appeared to dash any national title hopes. That ended up not being the case, though. After beating Alabama in the SEC title game, Florida got another chance at Florida State in the Sugar Bowl.

This time, Florida was ready. Senior quarterback Danny Wuerffel and junior wide receiver Ike Hilliard starred. The pair hooked up for seven receptions, 150 yards, and three touchdowns. Florida held a seven-point lead at halftime. And the Gators then scored four unanswered touchdowns in the second half. The result was a 52–20 win. Florida had finally won its first national title.

Florida did not win another national title until 2006. But the Gators continued to be a force in college football. They won 29 of their next 34 games. They also remained in the top 10 in the country nearly every week for the rest of the decade.

Spurrier's coaching abilities had not gone unnoticed. The NFL's Washington Redskins hired him away in 2002. Former Florida assistant coach Ron Zook replaced him.

The Gators took a step back under Zook. They lost five games in each of his three years as coach. They also struggled to put away opponents. Florida blew fourth-quarter leads to Miami, Mississippi, and Florida State in 2003. They then lost fourth-quarter leads to Tennessee and Louisiana State University in 2004. The last straw was an embarrassing 38–31 loss to Mississippi State in 2004. Zook was fired after that.

TALE OF TEBOW

In 2007, Florida quarterback Tim Tebow became the first sophomore to win the Heisman Trophy. As a Gator, he helped Florida win the 2006 and 2008 national titles. Many consider him to be one of the greatest college quarterbacks ever. Yet many experts questioned if Tebow would be a good NFL quarterback. Much of his college success was due to his rushing abilities. However, professional quarterbacks do not run as often as college quarterbacks.

Still, the Denver Broncos selected Tebow in the first round of the 2010 NFL Draft. Tebow became the starter midway through his second season. And he started winning. The wins were not always pretty, but Tebow led the Broncos to the playoffs. Even so, the team traded him to the New York Jets after the season.

Tebow also became very popular off the field. Some fans loved the way he conducted himself and that he was outspoken about his Christian beliefs.

Charlie Strong finished out the year while the school searched for his replacement. Many hoped that Spurrier would return to save the program. Instead, Florida went elsewhere. And the program would soon reach even greater success.

Urban Meyer had just guided Utah to a 12–0 record. Several top football teams wanted to hire him. Among those schools was Notre Dame. But Meyer decided to go to Florida. The school gave him a seven-year contract for $14 million. Florida fans hoped Meyer could bring top players and national titles back to Gainesville. And Meyer did both almost immediately. The Gators won their second national title after the 2006 season with the win over Ohio State.

The national title was a high point for the program. But the Gators would soon find even more success. Much of that was due

Florida quarterback Tim Tebow gets high-fives from fans after a 2007 game against Tennessee.

to quarterback Tim Tebow. He had played a spot role in the national championship win as a freshman. After becoming the starter in 2007, Tebow blossomed into perhaps the greatest college football player ever.

Tebow passed and rushed for 42 total touchdowns in 2008. The offense also featured junior wide receiver Percy Harvin and sophomore center Maurkice Pouncey. Sophomore cornerback Joe Haden led the defense. All later became NFL standouts.

The Gators scored 45 points per game in winning the SEC title. They swept through the regular season with a 12–1 record. That set up a showdown with Oklahoma in the BCS National Championship Game.

THE CHAMPIONSHIP ERA

Florida cornerback Joe Haden dives to intercept a pass during a 2009 game against Florida State.

The Sooners could not stop Tebow. He threw for 231 yards and ran for 109 more. He tossed two touchdown passes. His touchdown pass to junior wide receiver David Nelson with three minutes left sealed the game. Harvin also starred in the 24–14 win. He combined for 171 total yards and added a touchdown.

THE BEN HILL GRIFFIN SWAMP?

The Gators' home stadium is nicknamed "The Swamp." The name is a reference to the swampland in the Florida area. But the stadium's official name was Florida Field until 1989. That is when it was renamed Ben Hill Griffin Stadium. Ben Hill Griffin attended the school in the early 1930s. He gained tremendous wealth in the citrus, packaging, and cattle businesses. He invested millions of dollars in the University of Florida. His positive influence motivated the school to change the name of the stadium in his honor.

Florida's defense played a big role in the win, as well. Oklahoma had averaged 54 points per game that season. And the Sooners had scored more than 60 points in each of their previous five games. But Sooners quarterback Sam Bradford was held to just two touchdown passes that day. Meanwhile, Florida intercepted him twice.

Florida was the top-ranked team for much of Tebow's senior season in 2009. But conference foe Alabama bested the Gators in the SEC title game. Tebow still left on a high note with a 51–24 win over Cincinnati in the Sugar Bowl.

The Gators remained a strong team after Tebow—just not as strong. They finished 8–5 in 2010. Meyer retired after that season to spend more time with his family. Will Muschamp took over after that and led the Gators to a 7–6 season in 2011.

Yet the program continued to thrive. The long battle to establish the Florida football team as a consistent national title threat was over. The Gators had won that battle.

Florida Agricultural College plays its first football game on November 22 and loses to Stetson College 6–0.

The University of Florida adopts the Gators nickname for its sports teams.

The Gators bottom out with a 0–5 record and score just three points all season.

The Gators let an unbeaten season slip away with a 13–12 loss to Tennessee on December 8.

Florida joins the new SEC.

1901　　1908　　1916　　1928　　1933

An NCAA investigation cites the football program for 107 violations. Pell is fired after three games. New coach Galen Hall also has trouble with the NCAA.

The Gators become the first team in college football history to qualify for a bowl game after a winless season.

Florida goes winless in its first season under Charley Pell.

Former Gators quarterback Spurrier is named coach on December 31. His first season in charge is 1990.

Florida clinches its first national title on January 2 with a 52–20 defeat of Florida State in the Sugar Bowl.

1979　　1980　　1984　　1989　　1997

Bob Woodruff is hired as coach on January 6 and begins to turn around the struggling Gators.

A new era begins as Ray Graves is named the new coach.

Quarterback Steve Spurrier leads the Gators to a 9–2 record and a 27–12 Orange Bowl win over Georgia Tech on January 2.

Doug Dickey is hired as coach in January.

The Gators win seven of their first eight games but lose three of their next four to ruin a promising season.

1950   1960   1967   1970   1974

Spurrier leaves as coach in January and is replaced by Ron Zook.

Zook is fired after an embarrassing loss to Mississippi State on October 23. Urban Meyer is named the new Florida coach on December 4.

Florida upsets Ohio State 41–14 in the BCS National Championship game on January 8.

The Gators beat Oklahoma 24–14 on January 8 for their second national title in three years.

Meyer steps down as coach on December 8, citing health concerns and a desire to spend more time with his family.

2002   2004   2007   2009   2010

QUICK STATS

PROGRAM INFO

Florida Agricultural College (1901–03)
University of Florida (1903–07)
University of Florida Gators (1908–)

NATIONAL CHAMPIONSHIPS

1996, 2006, 2008

OTHER ACHIEVEMENTS

BCS bowl appearances (1999–): 2
SEC championships (1933–): 9
Bowl record: 20–19

HEISMAN TROPHY WINNERS

Steve Spurrier, 1966
Danny Wuerffel, 1996
Tim Tebow, 2007

KEY PLAYERS
(POSITION[S]; SEASONS WITH TEAM)

Carlos Alvarez (WR; 1969–71)
Wes Chandler (WR; 1974–77)
Cris Collinsworth (WR; 1977–80)
Percy Harvin (WR; 2006–08)
Jevon Kearse (LB; 1996–98)
Charlie LaPradd (OL-DL; 1950–52)

Wilber Marshall (DL; 1980–83)
Emmitt Smith (RB; 1987–89)
Steve Spurrier (QB; 1964–66)
Tim Tebow (QB; 2006–09)
Dale Van Sickel (WR; 1927–29)
Danny Wuerffel (QB; 1993–96)
Jack Youngblood (DE; 1968–70)

KEY COACHES

Urban Meyer (2005–10):
    65–15; 5–1 (bowl games)
Steve Spurrier (1990–2001):
    122–27–1; 6–5 (bowl games)

HOME STADIUM

Florida Field/Ben Hill Griffin Stadium
    (1930–)

* All statistics through 2011 season

In December 1912, the Gators traveled to Cuba to play a game. When the officials failed to call a penalty, Florida coach G. E. Pyle angrily removed his team from the field. The Gators were forced to forfeit and Pyle was arrested. The case never went to trial. Pyle and the Gators sneaked out of the country by boat and sailed back to Florida.

In the early 1900s, the Gators played their home games at Fleming Field. The Florida baseball team and track-and-field squads also competed there. The football team played in front of fans sitting on the hoods of their cars parked along the sidelines.

"I've often been asked, 'What's the difference between winning and losing?' Let me give you an example. In 1950 we lost to Vanderbilt. When the fans came out to meet us at the airfield, they took us back to campus in convertibles. Two games later we went to Kentucky and got clobbered. This time . . . they picked us up in some old yellow school buses, and we had two flat tires." —Red Mitchum, Gators offensive tackle from 1950 to 1951

"Call me arrogant, cocky, crybaby, whiner, or whatever names you like. At least they're not calling us losers anymore. If people like you too much, it's probably because they're beating you." —Steve Spurrier, Florida's coach from 1990 to 2001

GLOSSARY

All-American
A player chosen as one of the best amateurs in the country in a particular activity.

athletic director
An administrator who oversees the players, coaches and teams of an institution.

conference
In sports, a group of teams that play each other each season.

contract
A deal reached between a coach and a school stipulating money to be paid and length of service.

draft
A system used by professional sports leagues to select new players in order to spread incoming talent among all teams. The NFL Draft is held each spring.

motivate
To cause someone to do well.

recruiting
Trying to entice a player to come to a certain school.

retire
To officially end one's career.

rival
An opponent that brings out great emotion in a team, its fans, and its players.

upset
A result where the supposedly worse team defeats the supposedly better team.

violations
Actions that break rules.

FOR MORE INFORMATION

FURTHER READING

Gainesville Sun. *Florida Gators: 2006 National Champions*. Champaign, IL: Sports Publishing, 2007.

Kerasotis, Peter. *Stadium Stories: Florida Gators*. Guilford, CT: Globe Piquot, 2005.

Robinson, Guy. *Do You Know the Florida Gators?* Naperville, IL: Sourcebooks, 2008.

WEB LINKS

To learn more about the Florida Gators, visit ABDO Publishing Company online at **www.abdopublishing.com**. Web sites about the Gators are featured on our Book Links page. These links are routinely monitored and updated to provide the most current information available.

PLACES TO VISIT

Ben Hill Griffin Stadium
Stadium Road
Gainesville, FL 32611
352-392-5500
www.gatorzone.com/facilities/?venue=swamp&sport=footb

This is where the Florida Gators have played their home games since 1930, though it was known as Florida Field well into the 1980s. It is where some of the greatest players in the history of college football have performed.

College Football Hall of Fame
111 South St. Joseph St.
South Bend, IN 46601
1-800-440-FAME (3263)
www.collegefootball.org

This hall of fame and museum highlights the greatest players and moments in the history of college football. Among the former Gators enshrined here are Jack Youngblood, Steve Spurrier, Wilber Marshall, and Emmitt Smith.

INDEX

ABOUT THE AUTHOR

Marty Gitlin is a freelance writer based in Cleveland, Ohio. He has written more than 50 educational books. Gitlin also has won more than 45 awards during his 30 years as a writer, including first place for general excellence from the Associated Press. He lives with his wife and three children.